CAN SOMEONE
TURN OFF
THE LIGHTS?

THE DARK!

WILD LIFE IN THE MYSTERIOUS WORLD OF CAVES

BY LINDSEY LEIGH

PENGUIN WORKSHOP

TO MY FRIENDS, FOR ALL THEIR SUPPORT AND TOLERANCE OF MY BABBLING ABOUT ODD ANIMALS.

W

PENGUIN WORKSHOP
An imprint of Penguin Random House LLC, New York

First published in the United States of America by Penguin Workshop,
an imprint of Penguin Random House LLC, New York, 2024

Visit us online at penguinrandomhouse.com.

Library of Congress Cataloging-in-Publication Data is available.

Manufactured in China

ISBN 9780593662595   10 9 8 7 6 5 4 3 2 1 HH

Design by Mary Claire Cruz

CONTENTS

HEY THERE! FOLLOW ME!

Welcome to the Alien World of THE DARK!

Through the gaping mouth of the cave opening...

Little Brown Bat

...through winding passageways and deep caverns...

...past the drips and drops of stalactites, you can find some of the strangest creatures you have ever seen.

WE LIVE HIDDEN AWAY FROM THE PRYING EYES OF THE WORLD ABOVE!
Cave Cricket
AND AS TIME GOES ON IN OUR ISOLATED WORLD, WE ONLY GET WEIRDER AND WEIRDER...
Olm
WE'LL SHOW YOU ALL THE WONDERS THAT ARE WAITING TO BE DISCOVERED IN CAVES.

What IS a Cave?

Caves are openings to the underground world inside the earth.

They have a cave entrance, where light can reach, but some of them go deep, deep underground to total darkness. Some of the animals that live in caves have never seen the sunlight.

(Most people agree that if a human can fit inside the hole in the earth, it counts as a cave.)

WHAT'S THE SUN? CAN I EAT IT?

UGH, HUMANS... IT'S ALWAYS ABOUT THEM!

Grotto Salamander

Many caves are formed when water slowly dissolves a type of rock called limestone. Limestone is soluble (dissolvable) in water, so when water seeps through cracks in the stone, it dissolves the rock and forms underground pockets in the earth that become caves.

The type of landscapes that are formed by limestone are called karst. There are certain areas of the world that have more karst landscapes, and therefore more caves.

Cave

Soil

Aquifer

Because the water seeps through the karst landscape like Swiss cheese, water seeps through and into underground rivers called aquifers (a body of rock and soil that holds water), which can provide drinking water to people.

Many caves are formed from limestone, but some are formed from lava or ice!

Captivated by Caves

The study of caves is called speleology (speel-ee-OL-oh-gee), and someone who studies caves is called a speleologist! Exploring caves for a fun hobby is called spelunking. Some amateur cave explorers have even discovered new caves completely by accident!

Types of Caves

Limestone Caves

These are caves that are formed by water seeping through rock, also known as a karst cave.

Lava Caves

Lava tubes form after lava has flowed near the surface of the earth, leaving an empty space behind.

Sea Caves

Sea caves form along the coast, where strong waves carve out a cave in the rock over many years.

Glacier Caves and Ice Caves

Glacier caves are created when water from a glacier (a big, slow-moving body of ice) melts to form caves in the ice, but ice caves are rock caves that contain ice all year round.

Cave Structures

There are many types of cave structures, also called speleothems (speel-ee-oh-thems) that form when water containing minerals drips, drops, and flows over the cave surface.

Drip...drop...drip...The water droplets in caves, which are full of a mineral called calcite, fall from the ceiling, forming stalactites. The buildup of the calcite-filled water droplets on the floor create stalagmites. (To remember the difference, stalactites hang TIGHT to the cave ceiling.)

COLUMNS form when a stalagmite and a stalactite grow so much that they merge together.

CURTAINS form when water trickles down, causing a sheet of calcite to drape down from the ceiling like a curtain.

SODA STRAWS are formed by water leaking through cracks in the ceiling. Hollow tubes form that are shaped like, well, soda straws!

CAVE POPCORN are small nubby structures that form when water seeps from the limestone wall or when water splashes on the floor. (Don't try to munch on cave popcorn or you'll break your teeth!)

SNOTTITES are tiny stalactites that look exactly like their name...like snot! But rather than mucus, these stalactites are actually colonies of bacteria that drip sulfuric acid (a type of chemical that can cause third-degree burns to an unsuspecting cave explorer!).

CAVE FLOWERS aren't real flowers. They're made of gypsum crystal that slowly pushes out of dry cave walls.

FLOWSTONE forms sheets of calcite on the floor that look like goopy melted caramel.

RIMSTONE dams are step-like structures that form when water flows over an edge.

CAVE PEARLS are formed when water moves too quickly to form a stalagmite. They can be tiny, like real pearls, or as large as a volleyball.

Caves of the

Check out some of the cave-dense areas of the world and some of the caves featured in this book!

6 15 17 12
2
5
4 7
3
10

1. Erebus Ice Tongue Caves, Ross Island, Antarctica
2. Carlsbad Caverns, New Mexico, United States
3. Cave of the Hanging Snakes, Quintana Roo, Mexico
4. Ring of Cenotes, Yucatán, Mexico

5. Cave of Crystals, Chihuahua, Mexico
6. Devils Hole, Nevada, United States
7. Great Blue Hole, Lighthouse Reef, Belize
8. Kitum Cave, Trans-Nzoia County, Kenya
9. Krubera-Voronja Cave, Abkhazia, Georgia
10. Lava Tubes, Hawaii, United States

WORLD

RED
Areas with Karst Landscapes

11. Chauvet Cave, Auvergne-Rhône-Alpes, France
12. Mammoth Cave, Kentucky, United States
13. Movile Cave, Constanța, Romania
14. Son Doong Cave, Quang Binh, Vietnam
15. Sulphur Cave, Colorado, United States
16. Tham Sai Yok Noi Cave System, Kanchanaburi Province, Thailand
17. Tumbling Creek Cave, Missouri, United States
18. Veryovkina Cave, Abkhazia, Georgia
19. Waitomo Caves, Waikato, New Zealand

Types of Cave Animals

(The Three Ts)

Different animals use caves differently. Not everyone is able to live in the harsh environment of the cave, and various animals have adapted (changed to adjust to new conditions or environments) to spend more or less time there based on what they need.

TROGLOBITES: PERMANENT CAVE RESIDENTS

Troglobites (TROG-low-bites) are specially adapted to live their entire lives in the cave. They often are blind because they have no need to see in the pitch-black darkness of their home. They wouldn't be able to survive outside of the cave!

HOME SWEET CAVE

WE OWN THIS JOINT!

Olm

Mexican Tetra

TROGLOPHILES: Part-Time Cave Residents

Troglophiles (TROG-low-files) can survive without living in the cave, but they typically live in the cave for a part of their life cycle. They can leave the cave to go looking for food when needed.

WE LOVE THE CAVE, WHO DOESN'T!

Oilbird

BUT WE LIKE TO STRETCH OUR LEGS AND EXPLORE, TOO.

Spotted-Tail Salamander

Cave Cricket

THERE'S **MORE TO LIFE** THAN JUST THE CAVE, YOU KNOW.

TROGLOXENES: Cave Visitors

Trogloxenes (TROG-low-zeens) can pop in and out of the cave at will. Trogloxenes live in the cave at certain times, and then they can leave. They cannot live only in the cave.

Mexican Free-Tailed Bat

WE'RE JUST STOPPING BY FOR A SPELL, THEN WE'LL BE ON OUR WAY!

Z z

Caucasian Parsley Frog

Black Bear

Cave Animal Adaptations

It takes a very special creature to live full-time in a cave! Cave animals have unique adaptations to live life in total darkness where there is a scarcity of food.

SLOW MOVEMENT

Cave animals typically don't move very much, and when they do, they move very slowly. This is so they can conserve energy and go longer without eating because food can be so hard to find.

DON'T RUSH ME, I HAVE ALL THE TIME IN THE WORLD.

Olm

LOSS OF EYES

Cave animals often have tiny eyes or no eyes at all. This is because sight is just not needed in the inky, black darkness of the cave. Instead, animals use other senses to find food and mates like touch, smell, or sensing electrical currents.

Mexican Tetra

LOSS OF PIGMENT

Many cave animals are transparent or white. They have no need to be brightly colored in the dark.

Cave Catfish

COLORS ARE SO **OVERRATED.**

LONGER, SENSITIVE ANTENNAE OR OTHER TOUCH-SENSITIVE ORGANS

Creatures use long limbs to sense around the darkness of the cave. Touch is an important sense for cave creatures when their sight is reduced.

Whip Spider

Troglobites: Permanent Cave Residents

In Greek, *troglos* means cave and *bios* means life, which means that troglobites spend their whole lives in caves. It takes a very special critter to live in the cave year-round. They have adapted to live in a world of high humidity and consistent temperature.

WHY WOULD WE **EVER** WANT TO LEAVE?

Texas Blind Salamander

WE HAVE **EVERYTHING WE COULD POSSIBLY WANT** RIGHT HERE.

These eyeless wonders are perfectly adapted to spend all their time in the darkest corners of the cave, but they would quickly die if they ever wandered from the cave's safety.

Cave Millipede

THE Fearless
Waterfall Climbing
Cave fish

TROGLOBITE

These unusual fish (also known as the cave angelfish) can use their fins just like feet to climb up a raging waterfall!

They can move through a torrent of water and are specialized to live in the waterfall's constant cascade.

I'M OKAY!

THESE **FINS** WERE MADE FOR WALKING, AND THAT'S JUST WHAT THEY'LL DO!

The cave angelfish can climb so well because its spine and pelvis are shaped more like a salamander's than a fish's, and its pelvis helps it to move like it has legs for walking rather than fins for swimming.

Spotted-Tail Salamander

It's only been found in eight caves in the whole world, between Thailand and Myanmar.

The cave version of the Mexican tetra made its way from rivers into caves millions of years ago and has adapted to life in the total darkness. The surface-dwelling tetra is silvery and has sparkling eyes, but the cave tetra is pale and has no eyes at all!

I CAN TASTE WITH THE **TOP OF MY HEAD!**

The cave-dwelling tetra also has an assortment of odd features, such as having taste buds in some very unusual places.

Top of Head

Taste Buds

Lips

Bottom of Head

Gill Arches

TROGLOBITE

YOU CAN CALL ME A **SUPER TASTER!**

They also have more taste buds than similar fish from the surface world.

Not only that, but this fish has also adapted to the nutrient-poor life of a cave with the ability to survive with incredibly high blood sugar. This mutation would cause diabetes (a disease where the body is not able to regulate blood sugar) in a human, but the fish can thrive just fine.

It is believed that this adaptation helps the fish conserve energy when nutrients are scarce in the cave. By studying this fish, scientists believe they might be able to better understand ways to treat diabetes in people.

21

The Mystifying OLM

TROGLOBITE

The olm is a blind salamander that lives in underwater caves. Olms were some of the first cave creatures that were reportedly discovered in the 1600s.

When it rained heavily in the area, the rain would wash the olms out of the caves, and people at the time believed them to be baby dragons emerging from their lairs!

Though olms may look mysterious and foreboding, they really like... to cuddle!

TIME FOR AN OLM CUDDLE PUDDLE!

They seek out friends to cuddle with their incredibly sensitive sense of smell. They have such a great sense of smell to seek out mates without sight.

In fact, these cuddly creatures prefer to find a cozy spot with another olm, rather than be alone. They even enjoy cuddling with olms of their same sex.

Olms can live to be up to one hundred years old, and they can stay in the same exact spot for years.

They only move to seek out a mate, which happens once every twelve and a half years. Scientists studying one olm noted that it hadn't budged in seven years!

Salamander Showdown

Though olms look like another adorable aquatic salamander, the axolotl, they have a number of differences. Olms live in underwater caves in central and southeastern Europe, whereas axolotls only live in two lakes in Mexico. The olm also has a much longer, noodlier body than an axolotl. And the axolotl can see, while the olm is blind. But unlike most other salamanders that lose their fluffy red gills when they grow into adults, both the axolotl and olm stay in their larval form (a young animal that hasn't yet changed to an adult) for their entire lives!

Axolotl

Olm

Oodles of

There are many species of salamanders that prefer the quiet life in a cave.

Texas Blind Salamander

This cave salamander, which resembles a shorter version of an olm, has only tiny spots for eyes and cannot see. It hunts its prey of small invertebrates (animals without a backbone) by sensing changes in water pressure in the calm cave waters. It is very rare and it's unknown how many exist.

TROGLOBITE

Other Cave Salamanders

Spotted-Tail Salamander

Sometimes known simply as "cave salamanders," these colorful salamanders are troglophiles, living both inside caves and outside in streams, forests, and rock crevices. They like hanging out in the entrance to the cave, where light can still be seen. They're great at climbing cave walls and stalagmites.

TROGLOPHILE

Grotto Salamander   **TROGLOBITE**

This salamander is the only known cave salamander that has a complete metamorphosis, which means it transforms from a different larval form to an adult animal. (In their larval form, they have gills!) The grotto salamander is found in the Ozark region of the United States, in caves with a spring or stream. They feed on insects that eat bat guano (poop!).

Larval Form

Adult Form

KOOKY

Crayfish are a type of crustacean in the same family as crabs and lobsters. You might know about surface-dwelling crayfish (or you may have even eaten some!) but there are also cave-dwelling species of crayfish. These crayfish lack the reddish or muddy brown color of their surface-dwelling kin and are usually a ghostly white.

Shelta Cave Crayfish

This crayfish lives in only one place: Shelta Cave in Huntsville, Alabama.

TROGLOBITE

SURPRISE! I'M STILL HERE!

A cave ecosystem is very delicate, and a gate installed across the entrance to Shelta Cave caused a collapse of the cave ecosystem.

As a result, the Shelta Cave crayfish was thought to be extinct for thirty years, until it was rediscovered in 2019 and 2020.

Cave Crayfish

Mammoth Cave Crayfish

This crayfish is from the renowned Mammoth Cave in Kentucky, which is the longest cave system in the world. They are troglophiles, so they can venture out of the dark cave to find food or mates if they really need to.

TROGLOPHILE

Southern Cave Crayfish

The southern cave crayfish can be found in Alabama and Tennessee and can live for over twenty-two years, four times longer than other crayfish. Southern cave crayfish love to snack on bat guano and other small invertebrates that make their way into the cave stream.

TROGLOBITE

Cave Bugs

Remipede

Not a centipede...not a millipede...
have you ever heard of...
a remipede?!

TROGLOBITE

These critters
are the world's
ONLY known venomous
crustaceans (invertebrates like
crabs and lobsters). They often
live in underwater sea caves and
cenotes (sinkholes) near coasts.

Like the feeding techniques
of a spider, the remipede
uses its venom to liquify
and slurp up its prey of
other crustaceans.

MMM,
DELICIOUS
SOUP.

Its paddle-like legs are used for
swimming (and in fact, in Latin
remipede means oar-footed).

WHITE CAVE VELVET WORM TROGLOBITE

The white cave velvet worm is a very rare creature. Not an insect or arachnid, they are ancient animals that have been around for five hundred million years! Though not much is known about this cave variety of velvet worm, surface-dwelling velvet worms have a blueish or reddish-brown color.

SCHLORP!

Surface-dwelling velvet worms are also predators (some of which hunt in packs) using specialized limbs on their heads like a glue gun to shoot out a sticky slime that hardens quickly to trap their prey.

Cave Diplurans

Diplurans (also called two-pronged bristletails) are a super-speedy invertebrate! They have six legs and are wingless, but they are not an insect.

TROGLOPHILE

BUG OR NOT?

Technically, true bugs are only species of insects that belong to a group known as Hemiptera (which includes cicadas, leafhoppers, and aphids). But sometimes people use the term loosely to mean any sort of creepy-crawly!

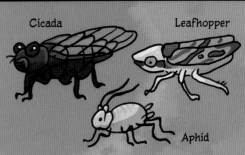

Cicada

Leafhopper

Aphid

29

IMPOSTERS!
Cave Pseudoscorpions

I LOOK LIKE A SCORPION...
BUT **SURPRISE!**
I'M A PSEUDOSCORPION!
NO STINGER ON ME.

(*Pseudo* means false.)

TROGLOBITE

Like scorpions, pseudoscorpions are also predators. Pseudoscorpions are also known as book scorpions because some types live outside of caves, in homes and libraries! Rather than reading, they prey on other insects that eat paper like booklice and dust mites, which love to eat the glue that was used in old books.

BOOKWORM?
NO, I'M A BOOK
SCORPION,
CLEARLY.

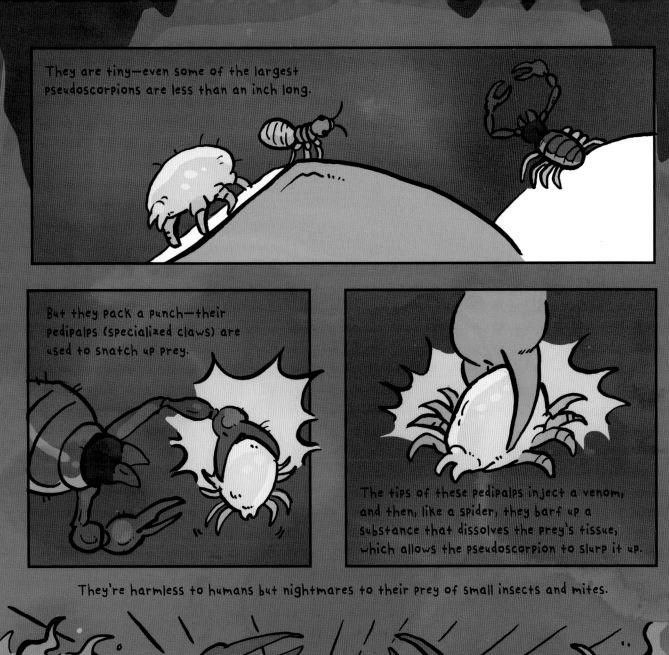

They are tiny—even some of the largest pseudoscorpions are less than an inch long.

But they pack a punch—their pedipalps (specialized claws) are used to snatch up prey.

The tips of these pedipalps inject a venom, and then, like a spider, they barf up a substance that dissolves the prey's tissue, which allows the pseudoscorpion to slurp it up.

They're harmless to humans but nightmares to their prey of small insects and mites.

Loads of Loaches

What is a loach? Loaches are a family of bottom-dwelling freshwater fish. In caves, they love to hang out at the bottom of cave streams and pools.

Xia'ao Blind Cave Loach

This long fish uses its specialized fins like legs to crawl along the bottom of cave pools. It is found in caves in south central China.

TROGLOBITE

Palace of the Dragon God Cave Loach

Not quite dragon sized, this loach only grows to about three to four inches long! It is found only in Guangxi Province, China, and was discovered in 2009. Very little information is known about this beautiful fish.

TROGLOBITE

and Cave Catfish

BLIND CAVE LOACH

This ghostly white loach has only been found in the rocky streams of one cave in the world (the Tham Sai Yok Noi cave system in Thailand).

TROGLOBITE

Cave Catfish

MEOW!

Catfish that live in caves are sometimes known, adorably, as blindcats. Like other cave fish, they have no eyes because they have no use for them. Instead, they use their whisker-like barbels to feel around their watery home.

Barbels

TROGLOBITE

One special type of cave catfish is the golden cave catfish. It is only found in one cave in Namibia. More than 250 feet under the surface, there is an underground lake where the golden cave catfish lives. It's thought that only a few hundred of these catfish exist!

33

Narrow-Necked Blind Cave Beetle

TROGLOBITE

The creation of speleology (cave science) is all thanks to this little beetle with a big butt!

These beetles were the first cave beetles known to science.

Before they were discovered in a cave in Slovenia in 1831, it was thought that no animals or plants could survive in a cave.

Like many cave animals, they are sensitive to humidity and prefer a humid environment. They also have a specialized organ on their antennae to sense humidity, called Hamann's organ.

HMM, THIS PLACE IS TOO DRY...

THIS PLACE IS TOO WET...

THIS PLACE IS JUST RIGHT!

The beetle's big rear end is actually its wings, fused together, because it doesn't need to fly around the cave and prefers to scuttle around on the ground, looking for its preferred food of bat guano and dead animal carcasses.

I'D TAKE THIS BEAUTIFUL BACKSIDE OVER WINGS ANY DAY!

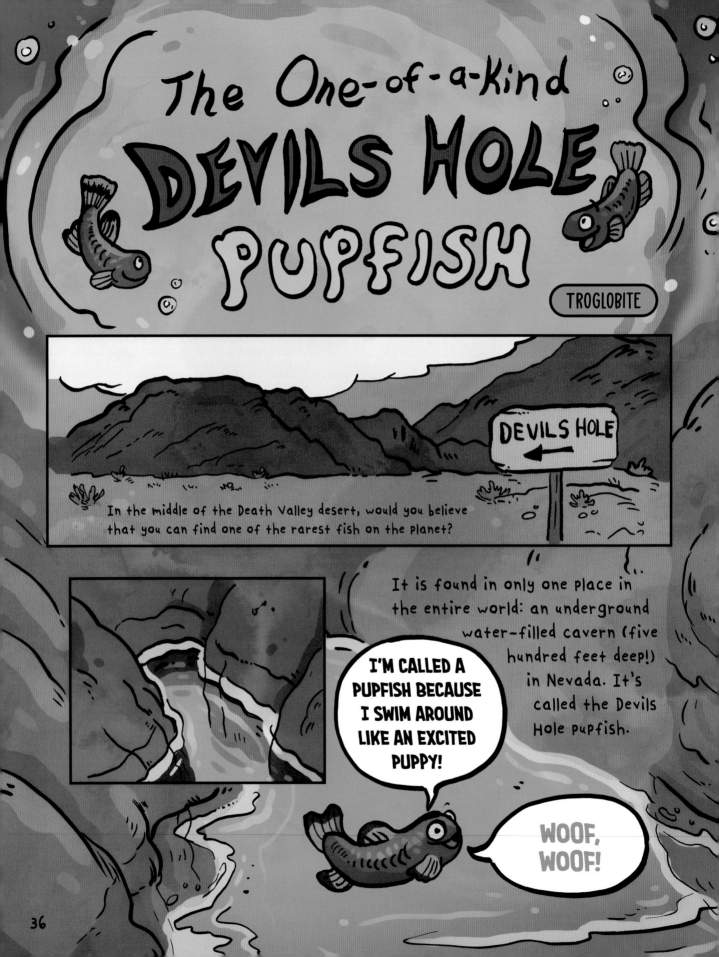

But how did the pupfish get there? It's not known for certain, but it's suspected that the pupfish arrived in Death Valley when it was much wetter, and when the water dried up, it left the pupfish in isolated springs.

They survive in such an isolated place by eating the algae that gathers on the rocky limestone shelf on the side of Devils Hole.

I'M A SURVIVOR!

But due to conservation efforts, their population has risen to 475!

The Devils Hole pupfish is very endangered, and in 2013, its numbers dwindled to only thirty-five pupfish!

Kauaï Cave WOLF Spider

This unique spider was only discovered in the 1970s.

TROGLOBITE

It is also known as pe'e pe'e maka 'ole in Hawaiian, and it lives in only one place, the Koloa Basin on the island of Kaua'i. And even then, it is found in only three caves.

Fewer than fifty of these spiders have ever been observed in the wild. The caves where this spider lives are called lava tube caves, which are formed by cooling lava rather than by water dissolving limestone.

Like other wolf spiders, the Kaua'i cave wolf spider carries its egg sacs and its little baby spiderlings on its back when they hatch!

HANG ON TIGHT, MY DARLINGS!

Like many other cave predators, it stalks its prey with its sense of touch. Its preferred meal is the Kaua'i cave amphipod, which is a small shrimp-like crustacean that also lives only in Kaua'i's lava tube caves.

LOTS of LEGS: CAVE CENTIPEDES AND

TROGLOBITE

You might find a house centipede scuttling around your home, but these leggy wonders can also be found in the depths of caves. Though *centipede* means one hundred legs, these centipedes only have fifteen pairs of legs, but that's plenty!

> I HAVE LEGS FOR DAYS!

Though the small house centipedes you find in your home are venomous, their venom only affects their prey of smaller insects. They're harmless to humans (even though they look a bit creepy).

The cave centipedes tap their legs on a rock's surface to visualize their environment and find prey in the darkness.

Another variety of centipede, called the Amazonian giant centipede, has also been found in limestone caves and has even been observed snatching bats out of the air to eat, which are much larger and heavier than themselves!

The deepest species of centipede ever found is *Geophilus hadesi*, a soil centipede that lives in the Lukina jama-Trojama (loo-keena yah-moo tro-yah-moo) cave system in Croatia. It was named after Hades, the Greek god of the underworld!

CAVE MILLIPEDES

Millipedes can also be found in caves, where they munch on fungi or decomposing matter. One newly discovered millipede in a cave in Sequoia National Park in California was found to have 414 legs and two hundred poison glands! Like many cave critters, it is eyeless and white. It's also very small, only about an inch long.

TROGLOBITE

Centipede or Millipede?

What's the difference between a centipede and a millipede? Centipedes are carnivores, but millipedes are vegetarians, munching on decomposing plants. Centipedes also have only one pair of legs per body segment, while millipedes have two.

Centipede

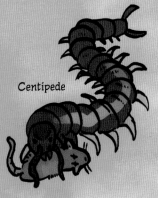

Millipede

The X-TREME Blood-Red Cave Worm

Deep in the toxic Sulphur Cave of Colorado live the blood-red cave worms. The whole cave smells like rotting eggs as it's filled with the poisonous gas sulfur (an element that is often found in nature).

These worms are extremophiles, which means that they live in dangerous habitats where other life wouldn't be able to survive.

They survive without sunlight, eating bacteria that munch on all the sulfur.

HOARDS of Harvestmen

Harvestmen (also known as daddy longlegs) are not really spiders. They belong to a group called Opiliones (oh-pill-ee-OH-nees). But they are a type of arachnid, a group which includes spiders.

Spiders have two body segments, while harvestmen only have one.

Spiders are also predators with venom, but harvestmen are content to scavenge for food and therefore have no venom.

HEY, GET YOUR FACTS STRAIGHT.

(There is an urban legend that daddy longlegs have powerful venom but that is just not true!)

They also have only two eyes, while spiders usually have eight eyes.

Eyeless, Cave-Dwelling Daddy Longlegs: Smeagol!

This harvestman species is named *Iandumoema smeagol* after the character from *The Lord of the Rings*! Just like the creature Gollum, this harvestman dwells in dark caves. It has no eyes, is a pale yellow, and prefers to hang out on wet cave walls.

TROGLOBITE

MY PRECIOUS...?

Bone Cave Harvestman

TROGLOBITE

The Bone Cave harvestman is only about the size of your fingernail, and it is a beautiful orange color. Like many cave animals, these harvestmen are eyeless and blind (so they can't see their own color!).

WOW, STUNNING COLOR!

THANKS, I GUESS?

CREEPY-CRAWLY CAVE LEECHES

TROGLOBITE

Discovered inside the incredibly deep and dark Velebit cave system in Croatia, the cave leech *Croatobranchus mestrovi* looks like a creature out of a sci-fi horror movie!

It has an unusual mouth sucker surrounded by tentacles, and it's unclear what these tentacles are used for.

The little finger-like structures on its sides are suspected to be gills so it can breathe in the freezing-cold cave water. It is one of the deepest underground animals ever found!

It's a mystery what these particular leeches eat in such an isolated place, but surface-dwelling leeches eat BLOOD.

Earthworm

Leech

Leeches are a type of segmented worm, related to the earthworm. Unlike an earthworm, they have a sucker that can draw blood, their favorite food!

Mouth

I VANT TO SUCK YOUR BLOOD!

Some leeches can eat ten times their body weight in blood.

I'M STUFFED.

After their feast, they might not have to eat for a whole year!

The TUMBLING CREEK Cave snail

This teeny tiny snail is only the size of the tip of a crayon and is known to live in one place: the Tumbling Creek Cave in Missouri.

(TROGLOBITE)

It is an endangered species and is threatened by sewage leaking into the cave and affecting the water quality.

EW...HUMAN POOP...NOT MY FAVORITE MEAL!

The cavesnail snacks on bacteria and fungi that feed on the bat guano that rains down from the bats that live in the cave.

The more bat guano there is, the more bacteria and fungi cover the rocks in the stream, creating a feast for the cavesnails.

DELICIOUS!

The dwindling population of cavesnails (there are only 150!) depends on the health of the gray bats that live in the cave.

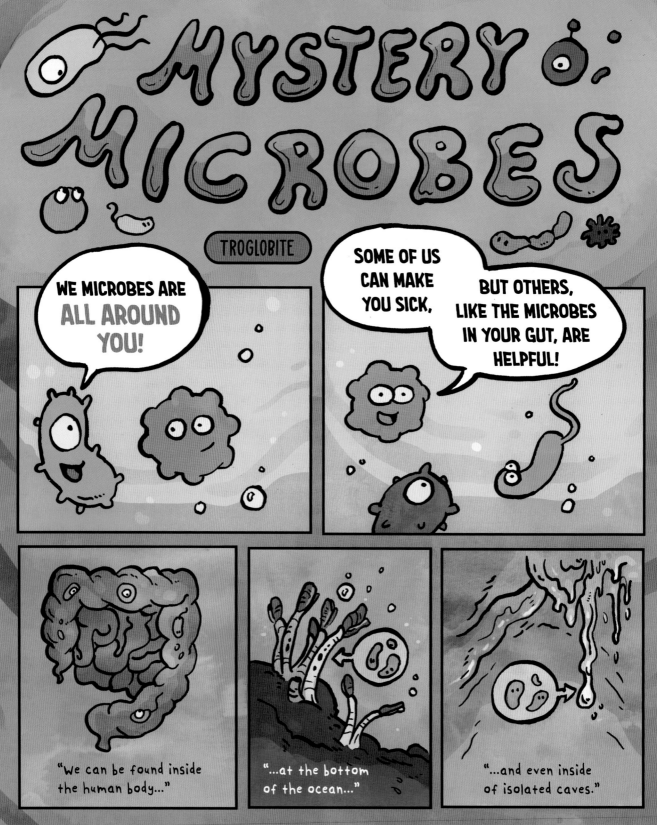

Bacteria in caves don't need sunlight to grow. Instead, they eat the minerals that are found in the caves. Huge microbial mats (basically a big sheet of bacteria) can be found in caves, clinging to the cave walls like giant globs of snot!

In Movile (moh-veel-ah) Cave in Romania, an entire environment filled with interconnected organisms (called an ecosystem) has developed around chemosynthetic bacteria, which means that these bacteria use chemicals, rather than sunlight, to create energy.

Just like in the deep sea where life springs up around hydrothermal vents (cracks where superhot water bubbles up from the earth), bacteria is the basis for life in the Movile Cave.

In the Lechuguilla (letch-oo-GEE-yah) Cave in Carlsbad Caverns National Park in New Mexico, the cave bacteria are rock eaters! It's believed that these bacteria munch on the minerals in the cave, which can even make the cave larger as they slowly eat it away.

Bacteria in this cave have also been found to be resistant to antibiotics (medicines that kill or stop bacteria from growing). By studying these microbes, scientists hope to develop new antibiotic medication. Learning about the bacteria found in caves could provide cures for new diseases as well.

The possibilities are endless!

GOT MOONMILK?

Moonmilk is a soft, white substance that is found on cave walls. When investigated closely, it was discovered that this substance was made up of different types of bacteria, algae, and minerals.

Doctors in the 1500s and 1600s would use dried moonmilk to stop bleeding and treat wounds. They didn't know it then, but moonmilk's antibiotic powers may have helped the wound heal and prevented infection.

The Glittering Glowworms

TROGLOBITE

IT'S LIKE A LASER LIGHT SHOW IN HERE!

WE CAN REALLY LIGHT UP A ROOM!

TROGLOBITE

Wow, what a beautiful night sky full of stars...but wait! Look a little closer. That beautiful starry sky is really a cave ceiling full of... glowworms!

Glowworms are not actually worms, but the larvae of a type of fungus gnat. Like fireflies, they are bioluminescent, which means that they can use a chemical reaction within their bodies to create light.

52

GONE FISHING...

They use their bright booties as the bait and their saliva, which they make into dangling, gooey, glowy threads, as a fishing line.

WOW, WHAT A BEAUTIFUL LIGHT...

The sticky thread ensnares mayflies and other small insects, which are the glowworm's meal of choice.

ACK!

One of the most well-known places to view these glowworms is the Waitomo Caves in New Zealand. The worms' gooey threads light up the caves with a brilliant glow.

DON'T TELL THE TOURISTS THAT THEY'RE ADMIRING OUR MUCUS, OKAY?

Troglophiles:
Part-Time Cave Residents

Troglos means cave and phile means love, so these creatures are all cave lovers! But they can also live outside of the cave. Some of them live only part of their life cycle in the cave.

CAVE TIME IS *ME TIME.*

Whip Spider

THE DARK IS SO **RELAXING.**

Cave Racer Snake

Many troglophiles still have their eyesight and pigment (unlike troglobites). Some members of the same species could spend most of their time in the cave, while others could live outside of the cave.

WE GOTTA HEAD OUT EVENTUALLY, BUT FOR NOW, IT'S **CAVE O'CLOCK.**

I NEVER WANT TO LEAVE...

Oilbird

Their fourth pair of legs are thin and long, just like a whip, which gives them their common name.

CRACK!

These thin, sensitive legs are used to feel around their environment.

A Mother's Love

Some whip spider species have been observed gently caressing their babies! A mother whip spider will sit in the middle of her young whip spiderlings, stroking their bodies with her feelers. The babies will even stroke their mama back!

LOVE YOU, MA!

THE ODD OILBIRD

Oilbirds are a cave-dwelling bird species, found in northern areas of South America. They are the only nocturnal, fruit-eating birds in the world!

They are called oilbirds because their chicks can get so fat that local people used to catch them and render them down into oil for cooking and fuel for torches!

Oilbirds spend their days resting in caves and then leave the caves to find delicious fruit to eat before returning at the end of the night.

They have an amazing sense of smell and nocturnal vision that allow them to find fruit in the dark (their fave is the palm fruit).

Once they've partially digested their meal, they barf it up to create their nests on cave ledges, then the female lays up to four eggs.

THEY'RE EATING US OUT OF HOUSE AND HOME!

The babies soon grow to a huge size on a diet of delicious, rich fruit.

Oilbirds make a myriad of screeches and squawks that sound like people screaming!

SQUAAAWK!

They can also echolocate (use sound waves to locate objects), just like a bat. The bird creates a rapid volley of clicks that bounce off the cave walls, alerting the oilbird to objects and obstacles around it.

JUST CALL ME THE BATBIRD!

The Creeping Cave RACER Snake

TROGLOPHILE

Cave racer snakes live in rain forest areas in Thailand and Malaysia, but they also enter caves in search of their favorite foods: cave swiftlets and bats.

Just by wriggling their slender bodies, they can climb without arms up the walls of the cave.

LOOK, MA, NO HANDS!

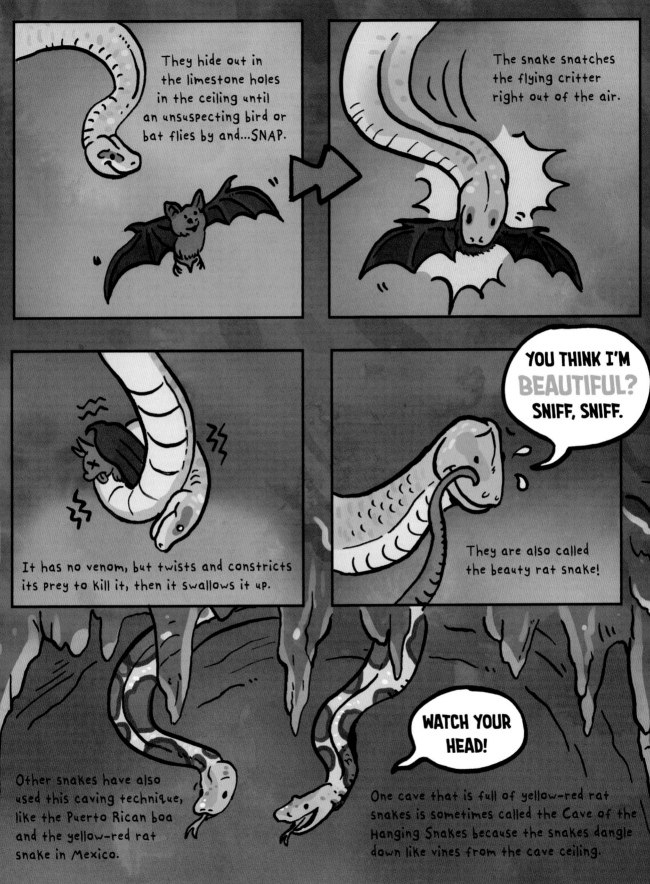

They hide out in the limestone holes in the ceiling until an unsuspecting bird or bat flies by and...SNAP.

The snake snatches the flying critter right out of the air.

It has no venom, but twists and constricts its prey to kill it, then it swallows it up.

YOU THINK I'M BEAUTIFUL? SNIFF, SNIFF.

They are also called the beauty rat snake!

Other snakes have also used this caving technique, like the Puerto Rican boa and the yellow-red rat snake in Mexico.

WATCH YOUR HEAD!

One cave that is full of yellow-red rat snakes is sometimes called the Cave of the Hanging Snakes because the snakes dangle down like vines from the cave ceiling.

Crawly Cave Crickets

TROGLOPHILE

This long-legged cricket shows another adaptation to cave life: lengthened limbs. They use their long back legs to spring away from predators.

They're also sometimes called camel crickets because of their humped backs.

These crickets are cave commuters! Every few weeks, they forage for food at the surface. They can eat more than 100 percent of their body weight in one sitting.

OH, SWEET GUANO! NECTAR OF THE GODS!

DON'T YOU MEAN POOP?

Then they bring those nutrients down with them to deeper parts of the cave in the form of their guano.

They are known as a keystone species, which means that they are very important to the environment of the caves where they live, including Mammoth Cave in Kentucky. Their guano is eaten by many other organisms like millipedes and beetles.

The crickets are in turn eaten by predators like cave orb-weaver spiders and the spotted-tail salamander.

IT'S THE CIRCLE OF LIFE...

Alien Invasion!

Cave crickets (along with many other insects) can be infected by a parasite called a horsehair worm. The worm develops inside the cricket, eating all the cricket's fat, and then it starts to control the cricket's mind! The worm alters chemicals in the cricket's brain, which sends the cricket toward the nearest cave pool (crickets can't swim!). The zombified cricket falls into the water and...*CRACK.* The horsehair worm breaks out of the cricket and slithers away into the water to infect another unsuspecting victim...

Trogloxenes: Cave Visitors

Troglos means cave and *xenes* means guest! Trogloxenes are cave guests that only spend a fraction of their time in the cave. One notable trogloxene is the bat, but raccoons, bears, skunks, and frogs also visit the cave for a brief time when they're searching for shelter in harsh winters and scorching summers. Trogloxenes are usually more colorful than the colorless troglobites, and they also still have their eyes.

NOT A BAD PLACE TO HANG OUT...BUT I PREFER WIDE-OPEN SPACES.

I NEED TO STRETCH MY WINGS!

There's another, less official group of cave residents called cave accidentals. These animals find themselves in the cave by accident, sometimes by falling in or being washed into the cave. They can't survive in the cave and will die if they don't get out in time! Their bodies will become a food source for the regular cave inhabitants.

Bats!

TROGLOXENE

When you think of a cave, chances are you also think of bats! But bats don't live out their whole lives in caves. Some species of bat, like Mexican free-tailed bats and gray bats, love to sleep the day away in caves.

QUIET DOWN! I'M TRYING TO **SLEEP!**

Then they fly out of the cave at dusk to hunt their prey of flying insects.

They catch these insects using echolocation (the use of sound waves to locate objects).

Many bats also use the caves as a shelter while they hibernate during the cold winter months (caves or other shelters used by hibernating creatures are called hibernacula).

The little brown bat is another species that hibernates in caves, though they have also been known to hibernate in man-made mine tunnels!

The world's largest known bat colony lives in Bracken Bat Cave in Texas. This cave is home to more than fifteen million Mexican free-tailed bats!

It is quite a sight to see the bats leave the cave at night in a huge mass, which looks like a ribbon flowing through the sky.

Such a huge number of bats produce a massive amount of poop. The piles of bat guano in the cave can reach sixty feet deep!

Ever heard the term "blind as a bat"? Just because bats have amazing hearing doesn't mean they can't see at all. Bats actually have pretty good eyesight (at least as good as people).

WHITE-NOSE PANIC!

Many bats in North America have been affected by a pandemic of their own: white-nose syndrome, which is caused by a frightening parasitic fungus. A parasite is an organism that lives on or inside a host organism and harms the host. The fungus latches onto bats' noses and wings. It affects hibernating bats, causing them to act strangely and wake up early from hibernation. When they wake up, there aren't any insects around for them to eat and they starve.

Bat Guano Ecosystems

Since there is scarce food to snack on in a cave ecosystem, animals will eat anything they can get their jaws on... including poop! In fact, some cave ecosystems revolve entirely around delicious morsels of bat poop that fall to the cave floor. When bats return to the cave after feasting and digest their meals, naturally poop comes next, raining down on the organisms underneath.

LOOK OUT BELOW!

A wide variety of insects love to chow down on that sweet, sweet guano. From beetles and cockroaches to crickets and mites, everyone wants in on the feast. (Guanobites is the term for animals that prefer to eat and live on piles of guano!)

THANKS, BATS!

WE'RE YOUR BIGGEST FANS!

All those insects attract larger predators, like the Caucasian parsley frog, which is a very rare frog species that lives in Russia, Turkey, and Georgia. This frog spends its winters in caves and prefers caves with a bunch of bat guano. The Caucasian parsley frog and many other animals are all able to thrive thanks to bat poop!

Tick Time!

Bats carry many parasites, such as ticks. There is one species of tick that specifically eats bat blood. These ticks have been observed carrying many baby ticks on their backs while walking over the guano.

WATCH WHERE YOU'RE STEPPING, MA!

69

SWOOPING Cave Swiftlets

TROGLOXENE

Caves aren't where you would expect to find a bird, but cave swiftlets have made caves their home.

Rather than the typical bird's nest material of twigs and leaves, swiftlets make nests from their spit! Male and female swiftlets use their saliva glands to create gooey fibers that turn into a glue that holds the nest tight to the cave walls.

When the bird's saliva is exposed to air, it hardens to create a sturdy nest. There are even differently colored saliva nests (white, yellow, or red) depending on what nutrients and minerals the bird has been eating.

Their nests are highly prized by people who use them to create bird's nest soup, a very expensive delicacy. People climb high up on bamboo ladders, risking their lives to snag the nests.

But the reward is worth it— the swiftlet's nest can fetch as much as $7,400!

More often now, people have created swiftlet hotels to basically farm the swiftlet nests.

The swiftlets have a safe place to raise their chicks away from predators, and people don't need to climb up the cave walls and risk their lives to grab the nests. It's a win-win!

WE HAD A LOVELY STAY AT YOUR HOTEL!

PLEASE FEEL FREE TO KEEP OUR NEST AS A PARTING GIFT.

Oh, Rats!

Even though they can live happily on the surface, the Allegheny woodrat enjoys spending time in caves.

VISITING A CAVE HELPS ME ESCAPE THE RAT RACE.

TROGLOXENE

Typically, these rats make their nests out of grasses and shredded tree bark, and they are sometimes called pack rats for their love of collecting shiny and colorful objects.

Their nests can be packed with everything from candy wrappers and bits of paper to corncobs and rusty nails!

JEEZ, MOM, THIS NEST IS REALLY UNCOMFORTABLE.

HUSH, SWEETIE, IT LOOKS LOVELY.

The rats often make their nests in caves, but they need to leave the cave to find their preferred meals of grain, seeds, and fruit.

When they return and get too far inside to see, away from the light of the cave entrance, they use their long, sensitive whiskers to navigate the cave.

The rat will leave trails of pee droplets behind when it moves through the dark cave, which it uses as a scent path to find its way back to the surface.

MUCH BETTER THAN A TRAIL OF BREAD CRUMBS!

Cave Elephants?!

TROGLOXENE

A cave is certainly the last place you'd ever expect to find an elephant!

But the elephants of western Kenya sometimes go deep into the nearby Kitum Cave in Mount Elgon, which is an extinct volcano, to eat salt if they can't get enough of the mineral from plants and soil.

At night, they make their way up a narrow trail into the cave. They can't see a thing, so they use their trunks and bodies to navigate the cave in the pitch-blackness, and the knowledge of how to get through the cave is passed down from generation to generation.

They use their tusks to scrape the salt, then gather the mineral-rich sand into their mouths. Their tusks even get worn down and stubby from using them this way.

It's believed that elephants have been visiting this cave for centuries, and during all that time, the elephants have made the cave even larger by mining and digging out the salt. Female elephants especially seek out the minerals during their pregnancy.

MOOOOM, ARE WE THERE YET? I WANT A SALTY SNACK!

Unique Caves of the World

Deep in a cave in Mexico, the largest crystals in the world were discovered in the year 2000. The cave is incredibly hot (136 degrees Fahrenheit!) with 90 percent humidity. The conditions are so intense that humans can only enter the cave for about ten minutes at a time.

Cave of Crystals, Mexico

Inside are giant selenite (a crystalized form of the mineral gypsum) crystals, some of which are thirty-six feet long and three feet thick!

These crystals formed due to the perfect conditions of the cave. The cave was filled with water, which was kept very warm from the magma underneath the cave, but when the temperature dipped, the crystals started to form. It is estimated that it would have taken close to one million years to grow crystals this large.

Movile Cave, Romania

The mysterious and ancient Movile Cave had been closed off to the outside world for five and a half million years! No human had ever even set foot in the cave before 1986. This ecosystem has flourished because of the chemosynthetic bacteria.

These bacteria thrive on the methane and sulfur found in the cave, and other animals in turn munch on the bacteria.

This way, there's no need for the sun or plants (just like how chemosynthetic bacteria can thrive at hot hydrothermal vents in the deep sea!). The cave walls and the surface of the cave's lake are coated in thick sheets of bacteria. It is also super humid in the cave, with almost 100 percent humidity!

Movile Cave is a twenty-four-hour weirdo party, full of extremely odd critters (who might just be a little socially awkward after five and a half million years of isolation...).

Water Scorpion

SO, UH, HOW ABOUT THAT WEATHER?

Some notable species are water scorpions, leeches, cave woodlice, and pseudoscorpions.

Pseudoscorpion

PRETTY HUMID...

Cave Woodlouse

THE FUMES ARE ESPECIALLY NOXIOUS TODAY!

Leeches

BREAKING CAVE RECORDS

Son Doong (SUHN-dong) Cave in Vietnam is the largest cave in the world (by volume). This cave is so large, it has a rain forest inside of it! Holes called dolines have opened in the cave, letting in light and vegetation.

The lush jungle is even home to endangered animals and a rare species of monkey called Hatinh langurs. Trees inside the cave can grow to be one hundred feet tall!

It also features the tallest stalagmite in the world, called the "Hand of Dog." Cave explorer Helen Brooke decided to name the structure the "Hand of God," but her partner misheard her and labeled it as the "Hand of Dog"!

Mammoth Cave in Kentucky is the longest cave in the world. Explorers have mapped 426 miles of the cave, but there are many more miles that are undiscovered!

The deepest cave in the world is Veryovkina (veh-ROV-Keena) Cave, but it is closely followed by Krubera-Voronja (crew-ber-AH var-OHN-yah) Cave. Both of them are in a region near the country of Georgia. These caves are deeper than six and a half Eiffel Towers stacked on top of each other.

Lava Tubes

Hawaii, USA

Lava tubes are deep underground passageways that form when lava flows under the surface of the earth. When the lava stops flowing, there is an empty space left behind: the lava tube.

How does that work?

1 Hot lava flows in a stream down from a volcanic eruption.

2 The top part of the lava hardens when exposed to air, but the fluid lava keeps flowing underneath.

3 As the lava stops flowing, the fluid lava drains away downhill.

4 The lava hardens completely, and the result is a hollow cave.

It has a brittle ceiling, which can collapse, allowing people and animals to enter it.

Once the lava cools, plants and animals move in! The roots of the ʻōhiʻa lehua (oh-hee-uh leh-hoo-ah) tree are first to poke through the cave ceiling. The nymphs (young form) of an insect called a planthopper move in to feed on sap from the roots of the tree. Thread-legged bugs and blind wolf spiders can also be found in the lava tube. These ecosystems are very fragile and are very easily damaged by humans.

Thread-Legged Bug

Planthopper

Kauaʻi Cave Wolf Spider

Cenotes, Mexico

A cenote (seh-NOH-tay) is a sinkhole, which is a hole in the ground that forms after water has dissolved limestone rock and caused the ground to collapse. Many cenotes are found in the Yucatán Peninsula in Mexico and are a very popular tourist attraction. You can even swim in them! It's thought that there are over six thousand cenotes in the region.

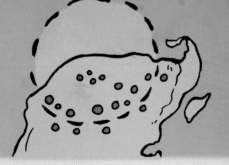

There is a ring of cenotes in the Yucatán Peninsula and the Gulf of Mexico around the giant crater left by the huge meteorite that struck the earth and led to the extinction of the dinosaurs.

YOU EVER GET A FEELING THAT THERE ARE GOING TO BE SOME **REALLY COOL** SINKHOLES HERE IN THE FUTURE?

Cenotes are fed by underground freshwater rivers and usually have cool waters that are so clear, you can see straight through to the bottom.

Some fish that live in cenotes love to nibble on people's toes, munching off dead pieces of skin.

Some animals that can be found in a cenote include:

IT'S AN **ALL-INCLUSIVE** SPA EXPERIENCE!

Cenote Shrimp

Mexican Blind Brotula

Blind Swamp Eel

Meso-American Slider Turtle

Crocodile

Glacier Caves

There are two types of ice-filled caves: glacier caves and ice caves.

Glacier caves only form in dense masses of ice called glaciers. They form when melting water runs through the glacier, creating a space inside the ice. Some of these caves form in Antarctic glaciers.

Even though Antarctica is frigid, there are warm caves underground that are heated by the volcano Mount Erebus. Some of these caves can be as warm as seventy-seven degrees Fahrenheit! These caves are home to mysterious microbes that get all their energy from iron or hydrogen.

The ice tongue caves of Mount Erebus in Antarctica are huge, full of dangling, otherworldly stalactites.

ICE TONGUE

The glacier these caves form in is called a tongue because it sticks out into the Ross Sea.

and Ice Caves

Ice caves are limestone rock caves that contain ice all through the year.

The Eisriesenwelt (ice-ree-sen-velt) ice cave in Austria is the largest ice cave in the world! It is a limestone cave in the Alps and is twenty-six miles long. The name of the cave means "world of ice giants"! The cave contains huge ice formations, crystals, and frozen waterfalls. It's even open to visitors.

Sea Caves

Sea caves are formed when the endless crashing waves slowly carve out a cave from rocky cliffs in a process called erosion.

Animals found in sea caves include invertebrates like marine isopods as well as gooseneck barnacles, anemones, sea stars, and sponges.

In California sea caves, harbor seals hang out to avoid predators.

and Blue Holes

Blue holes are huge, deep marine caverns (many of which are found in the Bahamas).

The Great Blue Hole in Belize is over four hundred feet deep and one thousand feet wide and is full of diverse creatures like sharks, sea turtles, and colorful fish like the midnight parrotfish.

During the last Ice Age, the Great Blue Hole was a limestone cave system. When the ocean level rose, the cavern's roof collapsed, forming the hole.

Just like we see in an aboveground limestone cave, divers have found stalactites and limestone columns inside the hole.

Human Cave History

Many animals have made caves their home, but millions of years ago there was a trogloxene you might not expect...humans! Paleolithic people (from the Stone Age, which began about two and a half million years ago) used to live in caves from time to time. They were nomadic, which means they moved from place to place a lot, and often used caves for shelter.

How do we know that humans lived in caves? Ancient humans left many pieces of evidence behind such as pottery, jewelry, and stone tools, but the cave paintings humans left behind might be the most beautiful evidence of all.

They used natural substances like charcoal, burned bones, or clay to create their paints, and then covered cave walls with huge depictions of animals.

One of the most beautifully painted caves is the Chauvet (show-vey) Cave in France. The huge cave paintings there, estimated to have been painted thirty-two thousand years ago, depict the animals that early humans interacted with, such as cave bears, cave hyenas, woolly rhinoceros, and cave lions!

Early humans painted the animals that were important to them in their lives, and these cave paintings have lasted thousands of years, even after the animals in their paintings have long since gone extinct.

THEY GOT MY NOSE JUST RIGHT!

I THINK MY HORNS SHOULD BE A LITTLE LONGER...

SPOTS REALLY SUIT ME!

91

Save the Cave!
Cave Conservation

Caves are delicate ecosystems that are very vulnerable to human influence. Humidity, temperature, and airflow can all impact a cave. Threats often come from the surface world above.

MINING

BAM!

Drilling in caves for minerals like iron ore can threaten life in the cave. Sensitive and rare species can be disturbed by the drilling.

POLLUTION

Pollutants dumped on the ground can easily find their way to the world below through water that seeps underground.

Aquifers (a layer of rock underground that holds water) are important sources of water for people, too, so they must be preserved for both people and animals.

TOURISM

Caves can be an exciting place for humans to visit, but people can change the humidity level of a cave just by entering it, which can be damaging to its delicate ecosystem. People can also leave litter in the cave and vandalize the cave structures. In addition, the noise of tourists can bother animals like bats.

FUNGUS

THANK YA KINDLY.

The white-nose fungus that devastates bats in caves can be spread by humans as they walk from cave area to cave area. The spread can be prevented if people clean their shoes and caving gear before entering a cave.

Delicate cave ecosystems are some of the most unique places on earth, filled with animals that are unlike creatures anywhere else. Caves are worth protecting! For more information on caves and cave creatures, visit the National Speleological Society website at caves.org.

INDEX OF CAVE CREATURES

Thank you to all the scientists and cave explorers who risked life and limb to locate and study these wonderful creatures!